THRILLING SPORTING MOMENTS

ROAD TO GLORY

Jeremy Daniel

Jonathan Ball Publishers
JOHANNESBURG · CAPE TOWN · LONDON

All rights reserved.
No part of this publication may be reproduced or transmitted,
in any form or by any means, without prior permission
from the publisher or copyright holder.

© Text and illustrations Jonathan Ball Publishers 2021
© Published edition Jonathan Ball Publishers 2021

Originally published in South Africa in 2021 by
JONATHAN BALL PUBLISHERS
A division of Media24 (Pty) Ltd
PO Box 33977
Jeppestown
2043

ISBN 978-1-86842-951-6
ebook ISBN 978-1-86842-952-3

*Every effort has been made to trace the copyright holders and to obtain
their permission for the use of copyright material. The publishers apologise
for any errors or omissions and would be grateful to be notified of any
corrections that should be incorporated in future editions of this book.*

www.jonathanball.co.za
www.twitter.com/JonathanBallPub
www.facebook.com/JonathanBallPublishers

Cover by Johan Koortzen
Design, typesetting and illustrations by Johan Koortzen

Set in 13 on 18pt Bembo MT Pro

Printed by NOVUS

Contents

INTRODUCTION   VII

CHAPTER 1 KEVIN ANDERSON'S EPIC WIMBLEDON   1

CHAPTER 2 BONGIWE MSOMI LEADS
           SA NETBALL TO NEW HEIGHTS   9

CHAPTER 3 LOUIS OOSTHUIZEN AND THE RED DOT 17

CHAPTER 4 LUVO MANYONGA LEARNS
           HOW TO FLY   26

CHAPTER 5 CASTER SEMENYA WINS GOLD IN RIO   31

CHAPTER 6 PERCY TAU STEPS UP FOR
           BAFANA BAFANA   41

CHAPTER 7 SUNETTE VILJOEN PROVES
           THAT WOMEN CAN DO IT ALL   48

CHAPTER 8 LUNGI NGIDI GETS HIS FIRST 'FIFER'   56

CHAPTER 9 CHAD LE CLOS UPSETS THE
           G.O.A.T. TO WIN GOLD   67

CHAPTER 10 TATJANA SCHOENMAKER'S
           OLYMPIC DREAM   75

CHAPTER 11	BLAST FROM THE PAST: LUCAS RADEBE WINS OVER THE LEEDS FANS	82
CHAPTER 12	CHESLIN KOLBE MAKES IT TO THE TOP	89
CHAPTER 13	ERNST VAN DYK – KING OF THE ROAD	99
CHAPTER 14	JANINE VAN WYK REMEMBERS HOW IT ALL BEGAN	106
CHAPTER 15	QUINTON DE KOCK TAKES THE GLOVES AGAINST SRI LANKA	115
CHAPTER 16	FAF DE KLERK STEERS A JAW-DROPPING SPRINGBOK COMEBACK	122
CHAPTER 17	AKANI SIMBINE RACES TOWARDS THE TITLE OF 'WORLD'S FASTEST MAN'	131
CHAPTER 18	BLAST FROM THE PAST: JOSIA THUGWANE WINS GOLD FOR MADIBA	140
SOURCES		147
AUTHOR'S NOTE		150

INTRODUCTION

Sport is all about thrilling moments. Sometimes, all it takes is a few seconds of inspiration and talent to change the course of sporting history. A kick, a pass, a burst of speed and courage that comes in the right place at the right time is what separates winners from losers.

Great athletes spend their whole careers preparing for when their moments might happen. Nobody can predict them. But, once in a while during a match, out on the track or in the pool, all the elements line up perfectly.

In the latest book in the *Road to Glory* series, we're highlighting some of the most thrilling moments in South African sporting history. Perhaps you saw some as they happened and missed others. Each of these thrilling moments counts as something that South African sports fans can be proud of.

Not every one of these moments led to victory; that's not the way sports works. But they all showcased the athletes performing at the peak of their powers.

What more can a fan ask than that?

CHAPTER 1

KEVIN ANDERSON'S EPIC WIMBLEDON

Why does it always have to be this hard? Kevin muttered to himself as the umpire announced, 'Game and fourth set to Mr Anderson. That's two sets all, going into the fifth and final set.'

Kevin walked off the grass, sat down and rehydrated as fast as he could. All around him, the fans were buzzing with excitement. For many people, a trip to watch the Wimbledon semi-finals was a once-in-a-lifetime opportunity and now that they were here, they were going to enjoy every second of it.

A long, tough fight was exactly what they had come to see.

Sitting on the other side of the umpire's chair was the American tennis player John Isner. Kevin knew Isner well. They had first competed against each other in college when Kevin had attended the University of Illinois. In 2007, he had been representing the state of Illinois in the championship dual match and lost to Isner, who was representing Georgia.

At the time, it had been the biggest defeat of his career and it had stung badly. But despite that, the men had become friends over the years.

Still, this was no time for friendship. This was the semi-final of the 2018 Wimbledon Championships, and a victory here would catapult the winner to playing the tennis match that every tennis-crazy boy dreamed about – the Wimbledon Men's Singles Final. It didn't get bigger than that in tennis, anywhere in the world.

'Time, gentlemen,' said the umpire and the crowd cheered. Kevin got to his feet, and immediately felt a heaviness in his legs. With one set to go, he would have to summon every bit of energy he had, to make it through. A few days earlier, he had played a gruelling quarter-final against Roger Federer. The match had lasted four hours until Kevin finally won the last game 13–11 in the fifth set. His legs were still feeling the strain and now here he was, about to start another fifth set.

The ball girl bounced two bright yellow balls to him as he reached the backline, and it was game on again.

Kevin's serve had always been his biggest weapon and he relied heavily on it to smash opponents. In the early years of his career, some people used to say that it was the only thing he could do. But he had never complained and had worked hard on all aspects of his game to become an all-round player.

Now he was competing to become the first South African to play in a Wimbledon final since Kevin Curren had, in 1985.

He slammed the ball and it ripped past Isner's racket. 15–0.

Kevin was annoyed that things had reached this point. He had been leading five points to four in the fourth set and had three set points but managed to blow them all and take it to five-all. He was furious with himself then and wondered if the tide had turned and Isner was going to steal the game from him.

Now here they were, with two sets each and everything to play for. As both men served ace after ace, game after game, they pushed each other to their limit.

The lead kept shifting in the final set. Both men were trying to find weaknesses in each other's games, while hiding their own aches and pains. Kevin could see that Isner's ankle was sore, and his own legs felt like jelly. Point after point turned into game after game, which turned into hour after hour.

Isner served the ball deep, onto Kevin's backhand. Kevin whipped his return right down the line, forcing his opponent to scramble a short return. That brought Kevin to the net, and he tried to finish the point with a gentle touch, but he overhit it slightly. Again, Isner managed to get there in time and return it.

Kevin made no mistake on the next shot and finished the point off.

As the game went on, Kevin's mind began to wander. He found himself thinking about what his dog was up to, or about some chords he had learned on the guitar. His mind drifted back to his school days in Johannesburg when he was known as a star 800-metre runner. He remembered feeling exhausted after those races but honestly, this was much worse.

Kevin forced himself to concentrate but his body was almost operating on autopilot. At one stage it was 8 games each, then 10 each, then they were at 12 and 13 games apiece. Every time one took the lead, the other pulled it back.

It was all about the serve. Both men were expert servers, and they took it in turns to win on their own serve and wait for the other to make a mistake.

They were two hours into the final set when there was a long rally. Kevin was waiting for an opening, when he was forced to sprint to the right, and he slipped and dropped his racket. Isner pounced as Kevin scrambled to his feet. His racket had fallen on his left-hand side, so as

He then flipped the racket to his strong hand and won the point.

the ball approached, he grabbed the racket with his left hand and made a decent return, then flipped it to his strong hand and won the point. The crowd went bananas!

Kevin glanced over at his opponent and spotted that his whole posture had sagged. He was leaning heavily on his racket. Right then, Kevin knew he could win this thing! Fate seemed to be on his side.

Still, the game carried on until it was 24–24. They had been on the court for six and a half hours, and the match had officially entered Guinness World Records as the longest semi-final match in Grand Slam history. Isner couldn't take it anymore. Finally, Kevin pressed his advantage, and Isner slammed the ball into the net, losing his own serve. All Kevin had to do was win his own serve again and that would be it.

He served beautifully in the final game and there were no sweeter words to his ears than 'Game, set, match, Kevin Anderson.' He was through to the Wimbledon Final. What a high

ROAD TO GLORY

point for Kevin Anderson and for South Africa! Whether he won or lost in two days' time, the semi-final would never be forgotten.

CHAPTER 2

BONGIWE MSOMI LEADS SA NETBALL TO NEW HEIGHTS

Bongiwe Msomi realised she would never get rich and famous playing netball. But that didn't bother her at all. On the court, she felt complete. She knew exactly who she was, what she was supposed to do and how she fitted into the team. That sense of purpose and place was priceless to her. Tennis players, golfers and swimmers might be more popular with the public, but netball was her sport.

And every four years, the eyes of the sporting world turned to the Netball World Cup. Now, for two weeks in July 2019, that time was here. Bongiwe had travelled with the Proteas to Liverpool, United Kingdom, to compete. It was a dream come true and she was determined to soak it up and remember every moment.

Looking around at her teammates warming up, she felt excited. They were a strong team. Sigi Burger, Lenize Potgieter, Maryke Holtzhausen ... they were all world-class players. With a bit of luck, they could beat anyone in the world.

'We may be ranked fifth, but I promise you, we're as good as Australia,' their vice-captain Karla Pretorius told them, the previous night. Bongiwe believed her; she could feel it. They were peaking at the right time and stood a good chance in this semi-final.

'How's the foot feeling?' asked goalkeeper Phumza Maweni in the changing room before the match. Bongiwe smiled and nodded. 'Not bad, thanks. I'll be OK.'

An injury had forced her off the court in the previous match against England and she had been worried that would be the end of the tournament for her, but her foot had healed fast.

'OK ladies, listen up!' said coach Norma Plummer in the changing room. 'I don't need to tell you how big this game is. The last time South Africa made it this far in the Netball

World Cup was in 1995. That's more than twenty years ago. I want you to go out there and play your best for all the netball girls at all the schools in our country. They look up to you and they know what you can do. Let's show the world!'

The team cheered and gathered in a tight circle, said a short prayer, and marched out to do battle against their old enemy, Australia.

Bongiwe looked around the packed arena, taking it all in. Sometimes, in front of a crowd, she felt as though she was in a dream. At Luthayi High School, netball had not been very popular. But her friend was in the team, so one day she went along to watch a practice. The coach, Thembisa Mncwabe, came over to where she was sitting.

'We're one short for a full court practice. Would you like to play?' she asked Bongiwe.

'I don't know anything about netball,' Bongiwe replied, but the coach assured her it was easy.

Now look at me, captain of the Proteas

netball team, Bongiwe thought, moments before the umpire blew the whistle and the semi-final began. The team settled quickly with a string of nice, clean passes. Lenize Potgieter took a clean catch and slotted the ball through the hoop. First blood to South Africa! That was a good feeling.

In every game, Bongiwe tried to get the ball into the shooter's hands as often as possible. The more times she could do that, the more chances they had at scoring. It was as simple as that. But the Australians were dangerous and tricky and getting the ball was not easy. The teams stayed level for the first quarter but then a few sloppy passes and turnovers saw the Australians move ahead eight points to seven.

As wing attack, Bongiwe saw herself as the key playmaker. She knew she had to dig deep and steer this team. But the Aussie shooter, Caitlin Thwaites, was a force to be reckoned with. She had a 100% shooting record in the first half and gradually, the Australians showed why they were ranked as the best netball team

Bongiwe tried to get the ball to the shooter as often as possible.

in the world. At halftime, the score was 31–23 to the Australian Diamonds.

The Proteas walked off the court feeling depressed. They needed something big to happen in the third quarter, or it was all going to be over.

As they walked back onto the court, Karla Pretorius reached out and touched Bongiwe's arm. 'Don't worry, Bongiwe. We're not out of this yet!' she said. Bongiwe nodded.

That's when things began to change. Karla Pretorius was on fire for the next fifteen minutes. She was reading the game perfectly, intercepting, blocking, and making life impossible for Australia. Suddenly, the Proteas regained confidence and the gap began to close. Three goals in a row from Potgieter and Maryka Holtzhausen brought them back to within three points of Australia. When the whistle blew, the score was 43–39. The crowd was going crazy, sensing that the biggest upset for years in World Cup netball was about to take place.

'Listen to the crowd,' said Pretorius. 'They're behind us to win this game!' And it was true. The crowd were screaming for the Proteas at the start of the fourth quarter. The South Africans responded well and quickly forced Australia into a held ball error. They scored a beautiful basket and suddenly the deficit was down to only one point.

The crowd was going crazy. Bongiwe's heart was racing but she felt focused and clear.

But there was a reason Australia ranked as top netball team in the world. Two crucial interventions – the first by Liz Watson and the second by Jamie-Lee Price – saw them push their score up to 50.

Again, the Proteas fought back, and it was 50–49 with a few minutes to go. Just one moment of inspiration could push them to the top. They did everything they could but, on that day, victory was not to be theirs. Caitlin Thwaites maintained her incredible record throughout the game, shooting 30 times and scoring every single one, and gave her team the edge. At the final whistle, the score was 55–53.

The South African team were disappointed but after a few minutes, they recovered. They knew they had given the game everything they had and done all they could. In 1999, Jamaica had lost to New Zealand by just two goals in the closest Netball World Cup semi-final in history; now South Africa had done the same against Australia.

Bongiwe was so proud to have been part of it. Next time, she thought, they could win.

CHAPTER 3

LOUIS OOSTHUIZEN AND THE RED DOT

Louis Oosthuizen was sitting in an office in Manchester, wondering what on earth he was doing there. Partly, he felt angry that he wasn't out on a golf course practising, but he also knew he needed to get his mental game right more than his swing.

'Karl Morris is ready for you, Mr Oosthuizen,' said the friendly receptionist. Louis got up and walked into the office. He had travelled up to Manchester that day to see the famous sports psychologist because he was convinced that his problems were more psychological than physical. He needed to get his mind on track.

They chatted for a while, and Louis answered the coach's basic questions. He was 27 years old, had grown up in South Africa, been a professional golfer since the age of 19, and he'd won a few important championships but none of the majors that he craved.

'Tell me about your last major championship,' the coach said, taking off his glasses.

'To be honest, I was all over the place at the US Open. It was embarrassing,' Louis replied.

'That's OK. It happens to everyone. Tell me about your pre-swing routine.'

So, Louis spoke about what he did and didn't do in the last few moments before he hit the ball. Morris asked questions that made him think hard about all the tiny decisions he generally tried to make at the last second.

Then Morris gave Louis some advice that would change his life forever. He told him that he wanted Louis to draw a small red spot on his glove and focus only on that spot when he started his swing. Nothing else was important at that moment.

'When you're about to swing, it's too late for thinking. Concentrate on the spot, clear the mind, and execute. Make it a ritual.'

LOUIS OOSTHUIZEN

Louis liked the sound of that and promised to give it a try.

At the 2010 British Open in July, Louis Oosthuizen was ranked as the 54th best golfer in the world. He was sure that he could rank higher, but he needed a few big wins to get there. Ever since South African golfing legend Ernie Els had spotted him playing as a teenager in Mossel Bay, he had been aiming for the top. And for a long time, everything had gone exactly to plan.

From 2004 to 2008, Louis had won five big tournaments in South Africa and was poised to storm the world stage. But playing against the best talent in the world every month turned out to be harder than Louis had imagined.

In every golf tournament the pack of players is cut in half after two rounds, and the bottom half are eliminated. In eight attempts, Louis had made the cut only once to play the final two days of a world championship. Making the cut was the very least he had to do to prove himself.

There was no better place to do it than at the 2010 Open Championship at St Andrews golf club in Scotland – the spiritual home of golf, where the game as we know it today was invented.

The very first time he teed off, Louis glanced down at the red dot he had painted on his glove with a magic marker and hoped if it would make a difference. Then he put his thoughts away and just started to play.

The first drive was straight and true down the middle of the fairway and Louis relaxed. He made a few more great shots, kept to par and started to really enjoy the game. When things were going well on the course, Louis didn't have a care in the world.

By the end of the first day, he was in second place, two shots behind Rory McIlroy from Northern Ireland, and one shot ahead of a pack of five players. He felt great and he really enjoyed the attention he was suddenly getting from other players.

Louis had an early start on the second day

and woke up wondering if his luck was going to desert him. But his first shot of the day was a towering drive right down the middle that settled his nerves. It seemed that the red dot technique was going to hold true for a second day.

'Brilliant, Louis! More of that, please,' said his caddie as he took Louis's club and they set off towards the hole. More of that was, indeed, coming. His putting was solid, his approach shots to the green were superb and his driving was inch perfect.

It felt strange to see legends like Tiger Woods and Lee Westwood struggling to keep up with him. Even yesterday's leader, the talented Rory McIlroy couldn't keep up with Louis. By the end of the day, he had shot a score of 67 compared to McIlroy's 80!

Signing in at first place, at the end of the day, changed everything. Now Louis Oosthuizen was the name on everyone's lips. People started looking at him differently. He was leading a major championship by five shots, with two days to go. 'Who is this kid?' they wondered.

Did he have the nerve and judgement to hold steady?

Louis knew that from here on it was a mental game. His only opponent was his mind, now. He was encouraged by text messages from old friends, colleagues, coaches, and even one from Ernie Els just telling him what he already knew – he was good enough to win the British Open.

The third round began with Mark Calcavecchia being Louis's closest challenger. But Calcavecchia's first five holes of the day were awful, and the American slipped right off the leaderboard. It seemed that the big players were continuing to struggle, while Louis's touch was as good as ever.

There were large crowds of people following him around, cheering after every shot – and that was a great feeling, but also created a lot of pressure. But he remained solid, scoring 69 for the 18 holes and maintaining a four-shot lead ahead of the Englishman Paul Casey, with one day of golf to go.

They were paired together on the final

Oosthuizen would become a powerful force in international golf.

Sunday of the Open, and the last to tee off. They both played a good par on the first hole, but on the second hole Casey tied himself up in knots and it took him three putts to finish it off. Louis just kept on doing what he was doing. His caddie played a huge role that day, keeping him focused and calm.

On the ninth hole, Louis had driven the ball beautifully onto the green. He had a putt of about 13 metres to make. He looked down at the red dot on his glove, took a deep breath, cleared his mind, and stroked it in perfectly. That meant a score of two, where it normally takes four to complete; known as an eagle.

On the same hole, Paul Casey took seven to finish. That was the end of his challenge.

As Louis walked down to the 18th hole, he looked around him, wanting to remember everything about this day. Suddenly, he thought of the South African leader Nelson Mandela, who was turning 92 on that day.

'Do you think Madiba watches golf?' he asked his caddy, who chuckled.

'If he doesn't yet, he will start now.'

Louis smiled. If it hadn't been for what Mandela and others had done for South Africa, he knew he wouldn't be playing here at all today. He lined up his final shot and thought about Madiba one more time. Then he looked at the red dot, blanked his mind and ended the tournament.

Louis Oosthuizen was on his way to becoming a central figure on the golfing world stage.

CHAPTER 4

LUVO MANYONGA LEARNS HOW TO FLY

Luvo Manyonga wiped the sweat off his brow as he stood at his mark and stared down the track into the long jump pit. This was the long jump final at the 2017 World Championships and London's Olympic Stadium was packed with spectators. The atmosphere was electric.

It was time for his second jump of the competition. His first effort had been red-flagged because he had narrowly overstepped the board. Luvo was desperate to make this one count. The World Championships was the biggest challenge of his career, so far. He and his coach had been dreaming about and planning for it for years.

Growing up with a single mother who was a domestic worker in Paarl, Luvo had known hardship his whole life. But he had always done exceptionally well at athletics and his first coach, Mario Smith, had set him on the right path. His first success came in 2009 at the African Junior Athletics Championships, where he won a bronze medal at the age of 18.

A year later, he completed a magnificent 8.19-metre jump in Germany, which placed him in the top ten long jumpers in history under the age of 20. Two fantastic years of competition followed, where Luvo seemed to get better and better. During that time, he won gold at the World Junior Championships in Canada and at the All-Africa Games in Mozambique and started to make some serious money.

But in early 2012, that all fell apart. People back at home began relying on him for money and he started to feel used. All the attention went to his head, and he started going to parties and experimenting with drugs. Before too long, Luvo failed a doping test and received an 18-month ban. During that time, he went into rehab and began rebuilding his life, but when Mario Smith was killed in a car accident, his life spiralled out of control again.

Luvo ended up missing four seasons and only got back into shape for competitive long jumping in 2016. In March of that year, he recorded a personal best of 8.3 metres. Since then, he had set the African record, and a personal best, of 8.65 metres at a meeting in Potchefstroom. If he could do that again, surely it would be long enough to win the gold?

After all the years of training, the struggles, triumphs and failures, it was time to graduate from African champion to world champion.

Luvo looked up at the leaderboard. American Jarrion Lawson was in first place, after a leap of 8.37 metres. Luvo's immediate goal was to fly further than that and land his name at the top of the leaderboard.

He raised his hands and began a slow, rhythmic clap that was picked up by the audience and began to bounce around the stadium. The energy from the crowd helped him to focus and gave him the extra lift that he needed. He concentrated on nothing but the next thirty seconds.

Luvo took off into the air, legs churning and arms outstretched.

It was time.

Luvo set off down the track, arms pumping, running faster and faster; then standing up straight, hitting his mark and taking off into the air, legs churning, and arms outstretched into the final lunge forward and the perfect landing in the raked sand.

Quickly, he looked back to see the white flag being lifted, which meant it was a legal jump. Then he walked over to chat to his coach while he waited for the results to come out. After a few moments, there it was – 8.48 metres!

That could only mean one thing: gold! Gold for Luvo and gold for South Africa. For a second, he just stood there and let his emotions wash over him. This life he had lived, with all its ups and downs, would never be the same again.

No matter what happened – he would always be a world champion. No-one could take that away from him.

CHAPTER 5

CASTER SEMENYA WINS GOLD IN RIO

Rio de Janeiro was everything that Caster Semenya had imagined it would be – vibrant people, beautiful beaches, mouth-watering food, and a laid-back lifestyle. It was no wonder that tourists flocked from all over the world to this Brazilian city. But in August 2016, Rio was even more exciting than usual, as it was the host city for the Summer Olympics. Thousands of athletes and sports fans were taking over the city for two weeks to participate in and watch some of the greatest sporting action in the world.

World-class athletes like sprinter Usain Bolt, gymnast Simone Biles and swimmers Michael Phelps and Katie Ledecky were there, too. All of them – including South Africa's 25-year-old track superstar, Caster Semenya – were performing with one goal in mind: to win an Olympic gold medal.

So, even though Caster was loving Rio, she was not there to see the sights. She was there to race. After all the controversy and gossip around her gender and whether she should be allowed to compete, nothing was going to stop her. The only way she knew how to shut the critics up was to win.

Caster had trained harder than ever in the months leading up to the games. Just a few months previously, she had won the 400-, 800- and 1 500-metre events at the South African National Championships. She felt that she was in the best shape of her life.

The women's 800 metres was one of the last events of the Games. While the other members of Team South Africa finished their events, received their medals and began celebrating, Caster kept her focus on the track and on her goals.

She knew that she had the physical ability

to beat her opponents; she had proved that many times. What she had to do was to get her mindset right. The coaches had told her over and over that that was the key. Usually when she lost a race, it was because the other runners were mentally tougher than she was.

As the flag-bearer for her country at the 2012 Olympics, Caster had been expected to win gold, but she had left her final charge too late and she couldn't catch up to Mariya Savinova, the Russian who had dominated the event during those years. It had been one of the toughest defeats she had ever had to deal with. She still found herself playing the race over and over in her mind. She was determined not to let that happen again during these Olympics.

This year, her whole family had come to the airport to say goodbye and wish the South African team good luck.

'This is your moment, Mokgadi,' her grandmother Maphuti had said to Caster before she boarded the plane to Rio. 'You're a golden girl.'

Having the full support of her family meant

more to Caster than they would ever know.

The Olympic 800-metre heats began on 17 August, three days before the final. Caster ran in the second race of the day, and she got through without putting in too much effort. She cruised to a solid victory ahead of Ajeé Wilson of America and Shelayna Oskan-Clarke from Great Britain. All three qualified for the next round.

The following day, eight women lined up for the semi-finals, all fantastic runners. But they were no match for Caster, who came in first, ahead of Britain's Lynsey Sharp, in a time of 1:58.15. Preparations were over and now it was time to give it her all for the final race.

Before the final, Caster walked out onto the track in her South African tracksuit and surveyed the scene. It was the second-last day of the Olympics and many of the officials and athletes were exhausted and looking forward to going home. But there was a still a huge crowd in the massive Rio stadium and they wanted to see a good race.

CASTER SEMENYA

Caster was drawn to run in Lane 3, with Kenya's Margaret Wambui next to her in Lane 4 and Francine Niyonsaba of Burundi in Lane 5. Those were the two women she had to watch most closely in this race. If she let either of them get too far ahead in the early stages, then ... no, she wasn't going to think like that. She was going to stay positive.

All the competitors were silent, stripping off their tracksuits, staring down the track, checking their laces and focusing on what they were going to do.

'In Lane 3, running for South Africa, Caster Semenya!' said the stadium announcer, and the crowd roared.

Caster raised her arms to acknowledge her fans, then turned and stared down the track.

For every athlete, there comes that moment when all the plans and the hours of training are just a thing of the past, and now it's time for action. On the soccer field it's the blast of the whistle, in the boxing ring it's the ding of a bell, and on the track it is three simple words: 'On your marks!'

Caster put her toe to the line and looked up.

'Get set!' She crouched down slightly, waiting to explode into action. The gunshot cracked and the runners shot forward.

Caster got away to a good start. She could feel that she was quickly making up distance on her outside lane. As the runners turned the first corner, they were each in their separate lanes but then they broke and headed for the inside lane, looking for any advantage and to settle into a comfortable rhythm.

Caster found herself in the lead, running alongside Francine Niyonsaba. The two of them set a sharp pace, followed closely by the rest of the pack. After 200 metres of trailing just behind the leaders, Margaret Wambui moved up on the outside, running hard to take the lead.

As the first lap ended, Caster glanced up at the clock. It was at 57.59. That was a good time, but not a great time, and she wanted to do better than that. So, she leaned in slightly, stepping up a gear, and the crowd roared their approval. Niyonsaba had seen the clock too, and she knew what she had to do. Anticipating Caster's move, she came back hard on the outside, passing Caster's shoulder, and opened a small lead. The rest of the chasing pack fell back, with defeat in their eyes. By the last turn, there were effectively only two runners left in the race.

Caster still had plenty of juice left in the tank so, as she got to the final corner, she accelerated, running harder than ever before. Her body responded well, and she put everything she had into the final fifty metres of the race. With that level of commitment, on top of so much talent, Caster steamed away from Niyonsaba.

By the time she crossed the finish line, Caster had smashed the South African record with a time of 1:55.28, and she was ahead of Niyonsaba by over eight metres – a huge victory.

A gold medal at the Rio Olympics! Relief and joy surged through her. The crowd went crazy, and Caster flexed her muscles and went

Caster Semenya strikes her famous victory pose after another dramatic win.

into her trademark 'cobra' pose. As the other runners came in one by one, gasping for breath, Caster reached out to them with an open hand and a smile. A couple of her fellow athletes refused to even look at her or just avoided her, but that was nothing new. She had raced all these women before, and she knew exactly how they felt about her.

Back in the dressing rooms after the race, Caster saw the British runner Lynsey Sharp being interviewed by a television reporter. Sharp had finished sixth, and she was complaining that competing against Caster was unfair.

'What's your excuse for the other four runners who beat you?' Caster muttered to herself and turned away. A few years ago, that kind of comment from Sharp would have hurt her badly, but now she felt nothing. She was an Olympic champion; no need to apologise for that!

Caster grabbed the South African flag that she had been carrying with her since the end of the race and drew it tightly around her shoulders. She knew that the people she cared about really believed in her. When she closed her eyes, she could feel waves of support all the way from South Africa crashing over the Rio Olympics.

CHAPTER 6

PERCY TAU STEPS UP FOR BAFANA BAFANA

Percy's excellent form on the soccer pitch was rewarded in March 2017, when he got called up to join the national squad, Bafana Bafana, in a game against Guinea-Bissau at Durban's Moses Mabhida Stadium.

This wasn't Percy's first game for Bafana Bafana. He had played twice in 2015 during the first round of matches against Angola in the African Cup of Nations but had made very little impact. Some people said he had blown his chances, but he had been patient and made sure that he couldn't be ignored.

Now, at 23 years old, he felt ready. He was in top form and felt sure that he could take his goalscoring ability to national level.

Bafana Bafana were being coached by Owen

da Gama for the match against Guinea-Bissau. Da Gama let Percy know that he would start on the bench, as a substitute, but that he hoped to use him in the second half, depending on how the match unfolded.

'I'm fine with that, Coach,' said Percy. 'I'm just happy to be part of the national squad. Put me wherever you need me.'

'They told me you'd become a team player, and I'm glad to see that's true,' the coach replied.

On arrival in Durban to meet up with the team, Percy was thrilled to bump into his old teammate, Keagan Dolly, at the airport. Keagan had recently left Sundowns to play in Europe. Percy had missed having the skilful footballer working alongside him and looked forward to playing with him in the upcoming game.

'Long time no see, Keagan,' he shouted across the busy terminal.

'Too long, Percy. I hope you've brought your goalscoring boots along,' replied Keagan.

On the short journey to the hotel, the two friends discussed what had been happening in each other's lives and Keagan told him what it was like to play in Europe, while Percy explained how things had got so much better for him, the second time around, with Mamelodi Sundowns.

Percy loved Durban. Once he'd checked into the hotel, he walked down to the beachfront and soaked up the relaxed vibes, before reporting for training.

A few hours before the game, when he walked into the changing room and saw the famous gold and yellow outfit hanging in front of his locker, Percy felt a lump in his throat. He was glad to be wearing sunglasses; at least the other players wouldn't notice his emotion.

Getting changed quickly, he thought about how impossible a game with Bafana Bafana had seemed to him a few months ago. His mother liked to say that sometimes dreams come true when you least expect it, and she was right.

As his team sang the national anthem, he promised himself that if he had a chance to play

GOAL! Two–nil to Bafana Bafana and Percy's first international goal.

later, he would make an impact on the game.

The visiting team started well, mounting attack after attack on the Bafana goals, but keeper Itumeleng Khune managed to keep them out. It was a nervous start for Bafana, but the team soon settled.

Thulani Serero collected a long ball through the middle, turned and ran hard at the defence. He was brought down just inside the penalty area and the referee pointed at the penalty spot. Kermit Erasmus stepped up to take the penalty, calmly stroked the ball beyond the goalkeeper's extended fingers, and scored Bafana's first goal of the match.

Percy sat on the bench for nearly an hour. He was beginning to think his chance wouldn't come. Then, the coach turned and signalled to him to get ready. He stripped down quickly and took his place on the touchline. The manager called for Erasmus to be replaced and Percy sprinted onto the field to the cheers of the passionate crowd.

No sooner was Percy on the field than a

chance presented itself. His team put together a series of beautiful passes, slowly working the ball up the field. Percy spotted a gap and ran for it, and Serero slid the ball into his path. Percy turned and fired low and hard for the corner and watched in amazement as it flew into the back of the net.

GOAL! Two–nil to Bafana Bafana and Percy's first international goal. What a moment! He ran over to the sideline, lifted his arms in triumph and was swamped by his teammates.

'You did it, Perce! You did it!' shouted Keagan over the roar of the crowd. Percy felt a wave of relief. Any nervousness he'd felt about playing at this level quickly vanished. He was meant to be here.

The newly energised South Africans pressed forward, earning another penalty, which Andile Jali slotted easily into the goals, and the game finished 3–1 to South Africa.

Later that month, Percy found a video clip of his goal on YouTube. He watched it over and over to remind himself that he belonged on the international stage. There would be no stopping him now. All he had to do was believe it.

CHAPTER 7

SUNETTE VILJOEN PROVES THAT WOMEN CAN DO IT ALL

To become an international cricketer at only 19 years old was a dream come true. Sunette Viljoen had been an enthusiastic all-rounder on the sports field since the start of junior school. At her high school in Rustenburg, she had played every sport that was on offer, and had done brilliantly in them all. But it was during the cricket and athletics season that she really shone.

Now, here she was, in 2002, fielding on the boundary in a Test match in Paarl against India. Sunette was rapidly shaken out of her daydream when the Indian batter, Hemlata Kala, drove the ball towards the boundary where she was standing. She ran hard to reach the ball, stretching out a foot to stop it only a few centimetres from the boundary, then turning around, scooping it up and launching it towards the wickets.

One of the reasons that Sunette had been put on the boundary to field was because her throws were so strong and accurate. The wicketkeeper stood up close to catch the ball but there was no need for that. Sunette's 25-metre throw was inch perfect, and it hit the middle stump right out of the ground.

Kala was nowhere close to the crease, and she looked stunned at the strength of the throw. India was five down for 314. Sunette had broken the 100-run partnership that had been crushing her team.

Later that week, she came to bat at number six and played one of the best innings of her career. Everything came together. She was seeing the ball so beautifully and the pitch suited her. She settled down with some great shots and soon she was scooping the ball over the fielders and reaching her first 50 for South Africa. With her score on 71, Sunette started to believe that she could score 100 runs. But it was not to be. A slow reaction to a fast ball from Bindeshwari Goyal had her bowled out.

Most people expected Sunette to carry on with her cricket career, but in her heart of hearts, she knew that this was her last series. She loved cricket but, more than anything, she wanted to be a professional athlete and compete against the very best talent in the world at the Olympic Games or the African Games. So, after the series, she made the difficult decision to retire from international cricket and focus on athletics, especially the javelin.

The 2004 Olympic Games in Athens were only two years away and Sunette was determined to qualify and do well there. But she knew that she had a far better chance at the Beijing Olympics in six years' time. Before then, there was so much work to do. She decided the 2006 Commonwealth Games would be a key test for her.

Her coach devised a varied training regime and they got down to work. Sunette didn't want to focus only on throwing, she wanted to build her all-round athletic ability.

'Javelin is really hard work because you need a lot of things. You have to be strong, you have to be fast, to be flexible, to be explosive; have rhythm, technique and co-ordination. There are a lot of things you need to work on, a lot of things you need to sharpen up before the javelin will fly,' she told a reporter.

Her gym routine was six hours a day, six days a week, with a rest on Sundays. Every day she did something different – hurdles, rhythm work, general throwing, shot put, sprints – all designed to turn Sunette into a gold-medal javelin thrower.

And then disaster struck. Sunette underwent a routine drug test and was stunned when her results came back positive. 'This must be a mistake,' she said, 'I've never taken an illegal substance in my whole life.'

The results showed that her hormone levels were too high, which could lead to a two-year doping suspension! She felt devastated and confused, but then she realised that her whole

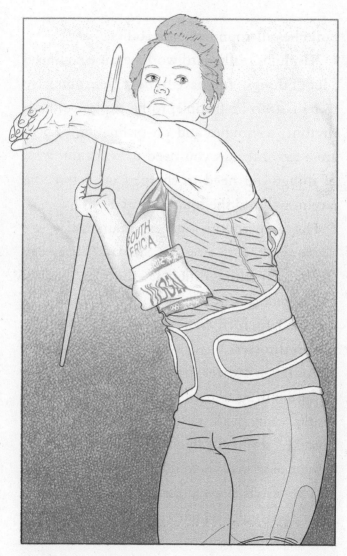

She sped up, drew her arm back and exploded into action.

body felt different. Something had changed. What could it be? A visit to her doctor provided the result.

Sunette was pregnant with a little boy. That was why her hormones were elevated and why she had failed the drug test. The relief was intense, along with the joy that she was going to be a mother. But there was anxiety too. To be a professional athlete and a mother was going to be that much more difficult, and she was only 21 years old.

In June 2005, her son Henre was born, and Sunette took to motherhood naturally. It was challenging, but it was beautiful, and full of love and happiness. But she had to keep one eye on her career, so, as soon as she could, she was back in the gym.

The Commonwealth Games were only eight months away. Few people believed Sunette had a chance of making the South African team. But she proved them wrong. She qualified and flew off with the team to compete in Melbourne, Australia.

ROAD TO GLORY

Some of the best javelin throwers in the world were lined up for the contest. In the first round of the competition, the Jamaican Olivia McKoy threw a big 57.04 metres, followed by Laverne Eve from the Bahamas who threw exactly 57 metres. After the first round, Sunette was in third place.

Sunette had worked so hard, as an athlete and a mother, and given up so much to be at the Games. Standing on the field, she gripped her javelin tightly and willed herself to win. This was her moment.

She started her run, sped up, drew her arm back and exploded into action. Everything clicked perfectly into place. The javelin sailed in a perfect arc and touched down gently. The crowd roared their approval and the referees raced over to mark the spot.

Sunette slowly put her tracksuit top on and kept her eyes glued to the scoreboard. There it was: 60.72 metres. A new Commonwealth Games record! Sunette was stunned and delighted. No-one would catch her now. Laverne Eve came close on her third attempt, but it wasn't enough, and Sunette took the gold medal.

Sunette was now a Test cricketer and a Commonwealth Games gold medallist. What an achievement!

CHAPTER 8

LUNGI NGIDI GETS HIS FIRST 'FIFER'

Lungi Ngidi was handed the ball at the end of the fourth over. Australia had already raced up to 27 for 0 losses in the second of three one-day internationals against South Africa, being played in Bloemfontein on 4 March 2020. It was a bad start for the Proteas.

'Come on Lungers, show them what you got,' said Anrich Nortje, thumping him on the back as he counted out his run-up and got ready to bowl.

Lungi needed to start off well. He couldn't afford a few warm-up balls. These batsmen were too good for that; the Australians always were.

Aaron Finch was facing as Lungi ran in and bowled a medium-paced, well-pitched-up ball.

LUNGI NGIDI

Finch stepped forward and turned it for a single. That brought the mighty David Warner to the crease, and he also scored a quick single.

On his third ball, Lungi bowled a bit faster but was slapped away by Finch for four runs. That frustrated Lungi, so he came in on the next one and again Aaron Finch was waiting and punched it easily to the boundary.

Ten runs off his first four balls. Lungi avoided eye contact with his captain at the end of the over.

Although it wasn't as though Anrich Norte, who was bowling at the other end, was having any better luck. He gave away 13 runs in that over, which brought the Australian score to 50. If they carried on at this rate, the game would be decided before South Africa even had the chance to bat.

David Warner was next to come to the crease and face Lungi's attack. Lungi was familiar with guys like Warner – tough, aggressive batsmen who sometimes became overconfident and underestimated what they could do with a shiny red ball. He ran in and sent a full delivery down to Warner, who tried to work it through to mid-wicket, but the fielder was there to stop it. Lungi felt good about that ball, so he dropped the next one a little shorter on the wicket and watched it rise. Warner swivelled and threw all his strength at the ball, expecting to see it sailing into the crowds. But Lungi had given the ball more bounce than Warner realised, and he almost missed it. The ball spooned up in a gentle arc. Dawid Malan got under it quickly and took a comfortable catch.

'Yes, Lungi! That's what I want!' shouted Quinton de Kock as the team surrounded him, giving high-fives and hugs. South Africa was back in the game.

Since he had been a youngster, the feeling of joy and satisfaction from getting a wicket had never changed for Lungi. Nothing came close to it, especially when he had managed to get one of his older brothers out. As the youngest of three boys, Lungi had hardly ever been given the chance to bat. The bigger boys all wanted

LUNGI NGIDI

to be Jacques Kallis or Sachin Tendulkar and they were in charge. He could only bat if he got them out, so he learned the art of fast bowling.

All that bowling made his back and his arm stronger, and Lungi realised he wasn't longing to bat at all. Getting wickets was far easier and more fun for him. Knocking over stumps was just as exciting as hitting a six.

Now the legend Steve Smith was coming to the wicket. Lungi snapped back into the moment. He had three more balls to bowl to finish the over and although he pushed hard, Smith was able to protect his wicket and survive.

After that, the game settled into a rhythm and the Australians began to pull ahead again. The Proteas were feeling frustrated. They needed something special to happen.

It was the thirteenth over when Ngidi lit the fireworks.

First, he bowled a beauty to Steve Smith that almost sneaked under his bat. Smith tried to dig it out but only succeeded in sending an easy catch to mid-wicket, where Jon-Jon Smuts

Lungi had his first 'fifer'. What a feeling to join that special club!

gobbled it up. Smith was furious with himself, and the home crowd went crazy with joy.

That brought Marnus Labuschagne to the wicket to bat. He had been born born in South Africa but now played for Australia. Lungi raced in. He dropped the ball short, and it jumped up high and fast towards Labuschagne's chest. Labuschagne couldn't help flashing his bat lamely at the ball and he sent it straight into a fielder's hands.

Two catches in two balls! A golden duck for Labuschagne and joy for Lungi Ngidi. He could almost hear the coach, Mark Boucher shouting in the dressing room, 'That's how you change the game!'

'You're on a hat-trick, Lungi! You've got this!' shouted Smuts as he grabbed Lungi in a bear hug.

Not only was it a huge wicket for the team. It was also Lungi's 50th wicket for the Proteas. He had achieved it in only 26 games, which beat the South African record for the fastest 50 wickets ever.

The Australians were reeling. D'Arcy Short came to the wicket. The fielders edged in closer, ramping up the pressure. The crowd was chanting and clapping in time, keen to see a hat-trick of three wickets in three balls. These were the moments Lungi loved about competitive, first-class cricket. There was nowhere else on earth he would rather be.

He fired it in, but it was too far down the leg side. The ball snicked the batsman's pads and ran to the boundary and Australia ran two byes. Lungi was disappointed but still, he had three wickets for 26 runs, and he had put his team in the driving seat.

Following his three wickets, the captain took Lungi off so that he could rest for a while before coming back as a strike bowler towards the end of the innings. Standing down on the boundary, Lungi looked around the stadium and reflected on how far he had come in such a short time.

Barely three years before, he had made his international debut in a T20 match against

Sri Lanka, where he was awarded Man of the Match. Then, a year later, in January 2018, he was included in the Test squad to play against India. He would never forget his first match with the Proteas, where he took seven wickets in total, and the team won by 135 runs. That same month he was bought by the Chennai Super Kings for a fee of one million rand to play in the Indian Premier League.

It had all happened so fast. Lungi Ngidi, the son of a domestic worker and a maintenance man who worked long, hard hours to put food on the table was suddenly in the international headlines. And now, here he was in March 2020, facing off against South Africa's oldest rivals in a one-day game of cricket in front of a packed, rowdy crowd of fans.

By the 46th over, Australia had scored 249 runs for 6 wickets. There were four overs to go.

'Lungi! You're on, next over!' shouted his captain and Lungi began to warm up his arm.

Alex Carey and Ashton Agar were batting, and they were confident about getting their team to at least 300 before the end of the innings. But they hadn't taken a fired-up Lungi into account. He was ready and hungry. He ran in hard and bowled a beautiful ball on middle stump that Agar tried to hit but it went straight to mid-wicket. David Miller was there for the catch, but he dropped it, then tried to recover fast and threw the ball hard at the wickets. No-one was ready for that, and it missed the stumps and raced to the boundary for five runs. Infuriating!

A couple of balls later, Lungi bowled an even better delivery, and this time Agar had no reply. He lofted the ball up high towards Keshav Maharaj on the boundary, who held on to it beautifully. Lungi had his fourth wicket.

Anrich Nortje took up the attack from the other end of the pitch and bowled a tidy over, only giving away five runs. Then Lungi was back in the attack and fired up to get his first five-wicket haul in a match, a 'fifer'.

He bowled straight at the stumps. The left-handed batsman, Alex Carey, tried to steer the ball past the wicketkeeper to the boundary, but it was too fast, and he grazed it into the gloves of the keeper, Quinton de Kock.

Lungi erupted in joy, then confusion, as the umpire's finger didn't go up.

'Howzaaaatttt?' he shouted but the umpire shook his head.

Lungi was certain Carey had hit it, so he asked for a review from the third umpire. Moments before they were due to review the footage, the batsman decided that he had, in fact, hit the ball and began to walk off the field. The umpire smiled and shrugged his shoulders at Lungi who grinned back.

Lungi had a 'fifer'. What a feeling to join that special club of bowlers! He felt like he could do this all day long!

And it wasn't over yet. Two more fast balls, then a slower one which totally fooled Pat Cummins, who sent up a gentle catch to Jon-Jon Smuts. Lungi grinned and shook his fist. He could hardly believe it. Six wickets against Australia!

Australia was all out for 271 on the final ball of the innings. The entire stadium leapt to their feet, clapping for Lungi Ngidi. His teammates offered him the ball to take home and stood back to let him walk off the field first. Lungi experienced pride he had never felt before.

On the scoreboard, three words summed it all up:

'THE NGIDI SHOW'.

CHAPTER 9

CHAD LE CLOS UPSETS THE G.O.A.T. TO WIN GOLD

Chad le Clos was ready to impress the world. The 20-year-old swimmer was at the 2012 London Olympic Games, and this was where he was determined to appear centre stage.

London was packed with fans, journalists and tourists as well as the best athletes from around the world. For the next two weeks, this was going to be the biggest show on earth.

Chad settled into the Olympic Village easily and soaked up the festive atmosphere. He was enjoying a reunion with his parents. His mother had recovered well from her cancer treatment, while his dad was bubbling over with excitement and plans.

Chad had prepared for the Olympics by watching, over and over, videos of races with the great champion, Michael Phelps. He probably knew those races better than Phelps himself did. In Chad's imagination, he was right there in the next lane, matching Phelps stroke for stroke and waiting to overtake him at just the right moment.

At a quiet restaurant the day before the race, his dad asked, 'So, what's the plan, Chad?'

'Gold.'

'Obviously gold. But what have you and Graham been working on in Monaco? Tell me everything.' Bert was referring to Graham Hill, Chad's coach.

'Chill, Dad.' Chad smiled at his over-enthusiastic father. 'My underwater swimming is stronger than ever. We're going to tie at the 150-metre mark, I'll match his underwater swim at the beginning of the last lap, then I'll go over the top in the last ten metres.'

Bert drummed on the table excitedly, picturing it all in his mind's eye. 'The underwaters. If he has a weakness, then that's it. Perfect!' he said.

'Your dad's been obsessed with the race for weeks. You know how he is,' his mom said. 'But Chad, I've never seen you this calm before a big race.'

'You're right. I am calm. It's a nice feeling.'

'It's because you've done the work, my boy,' said Bert. 'Nothing has been left to chance. Not a thing. And the best part is how Phelps doesn't even know you're coming for him.'

Chad nodded. 'It's almost like destiny. When I look out the window of my room, I look straight into the American team's rooms. Sitting and watching them takes all the fear away. Michael is just another swimmer.'

'Two arms, two legs,' Bert agreed.

The following morning, Chad went for an ice bath. Ice baths help swimmers' muscles recover after weeks of gruelling training. The ice constricts the blood vessels, which reduces any swelling. It also forces lactic acid back into circulation in the bloodstream.

He was surprised to see the Americans were booked in at the same time. Phelps arrived a few minutes after Chad, stripped down and hopped easily into the ice. They sat side by side and said nothing. Chad had a feeling that Phelps underestimated him as a rival, which suited Chad fine.

A few hours before the race, Chad and his coach walked towards the call room, where all the swimmers had to report and sign in.

'So, this is it, Coach. Long journey,' said Chad.

'Yip,' replied Graham. 'Whatever happens today, I'm proud of you, Chad.'

'Thanks, Coach. Any last words of wisdom?'

'No, you know the plan. You've done the work. So – just deliver. Try to enjoy it too.'

Chad smiled and thanked him, then turned and walked towards the door.

'Hey Chad! One more thing,' said Graham. 'I might be wrong but it's likely Phelps will retire from the 200-metres butterfly after this race. Realistically, this is your last chance to beat him.'

Those final words from his coach hit Chad

hard. If Phelps retired, then that was the end of a dream to beat the champion swimmer. It was now or never.

All too soon, the race was on. At the sound of the whistle, the swimmers bounded up onto the starting blocks and got ready. Chad pushed everything else out of his mind and focused. This was the moment.

'*Go!*'

Chad launched himself into the air, stretching his arms forward, and curved into the crystal-clear water, gliding and kicking hard for as long as he could. Then he burst through the surface, into his first stroke and away. It was a great start and Chad was neck and neck with both Phelps in lane 6 and Japanese swimmer Takeshi Matsuda in lane 4.

Chad matched Phelps stroke for stroke for the first 50 metres, and they touched the other side at the same moment, both turning at 24.76 seconds. During the second lap, Phelps began to pull ahead slightly, but Chad wasn't worried. He knew how much power he was keeping in reserve, and that he could catch up now if he wanted to, but the effort would tire him out. Stick to the plan.

At the halfway mark, Phelps was only 0.36 seconds ahead of Chad, with the Serbian swimmer Velimir Stjepanović just behind them in third place. The three swimmers were almost perfectly matched, stroke for stroke, metre for metre.

Then Matsuda came from behind and stretched ahead of Chad, putting him down into third place. The race was in danger of slipping away, but Chad dug in. He was ready to go, in a perfect groove, and he could catch up with both. Timing is everything at the end of a race. Getting the last stroke in at exactly the right moment, so that the swimmer accelerates towards the wall at full speed, makes the difference between gold and silver. With ten metres to go and the crowd roaring, the swimmers raced towards the finish line. Pull, kick, stretch, touch – the race was over!

Chad turned instantly and looked up at the

'Yesss!' Chad screamed, jumping high and slapping the water.

scoreboard. What had happened? It felt like a silver. But no, there his name was: Le Clos, in first place. Was he dreaming?

'Yesss!' Chad screamed, jumping high and slapping the water. Then he climbed up onto the lane rope, raised his arms to the sky and whooped, searching for his parents in the crowd. They were roaring with relief and pleasure. Chad could tell, just from the way his dad's mouth was moving, that he was shouting out his favourite word, over and over: 'Unbelievable!'

In the end, the slow-motion replay revealed that Michael Phelps had made a tiny error in the last few metres and left a gap for Chad to edge ahead by five hundredths of a second. That was all it took.

Chad le Clos had won gold at the London Olympics and stunned the world.

CHAPTER 10

TATJANA SCHOENMAKER'S OLYMPIC DREAM

Tatjana Schoenmaker touched the wall of the pool with both hands, swung her body around until her feet found the wall, then pushed with all her might. In an instant she was pulling hard and finding her rhythm, locking into the years of training and discipline that made her fly through water. There was only one lap to go – fifty metres – in the final race of the 2021 Olympic 200-metres women's breaststroke, and she was ahead.

The American swimmers, Lilly King and Annie Lazor, were pushing hard on either side of Tatjana, but she blocked them out of her thoughts and focused on the finish line. Her lungs were bursting by the time she touched the wall and she looked to either side. Had she won? No ... yes! Her thoughts all scrambled together, and she felt like she was in shock.

'Olympic Gold for South Africa and Tatjana Schoenmaker!' announced the commentator.

After a few moments of taking everything in, Tatjana looked up at the scoreboard. That's when she saw her time, 2:18.95, and the letters 'WR' flashing alongside her name. Still, it took another moment to register what had just happened. She had set a new world record for the 200-metres women's breaststroke!

The previous record of 2:19.11 had been set by Denmark's Rikke Møller Pedersen at the World Championships in 2013. Now, in 2021, Tatjana had smashed that time – the first South African to win an Olympic gold for South Africa in women's swimming since Penny Heyns in 1996.

She felt a wave of emotion burst through her and gasped in shock and delight. Then there were arms hugging her from all sides. The two American swimmers she had just beaten – as well as her South African teammate, Kaylene

Corbett – were all sharing Tatjana's joy and showing the world the true meaning of the Olympic spirit.

Tatjana could hardly believe that four years ago, at the 2016 Olympic qualifying heats in Durban, she had nearly given up competitive swimming for good. All her preparations for that race had gone perfectly. The pool was warm, the sky was clear and only a few weeks earlier, in Stellenbosch, she had already cracked the time she needed. She just had to do it once more.

On your marks, get set, go!

Tatjana had reacted well to the starter's gun, hit the water cleanly and was into her stroke in seconds. She was soon out in front of the other swimmers, but of course, her real competition was the clock. She pushed hard every step of the way, hit her turns well and made sure there were no silly mistakes as she touched the wall to finish first.

But one look at the clock nearly stopped her heart. She had missed the qualifying time by just one hundredth of a second!

She turned to look at her coach, Rocco Meiring, and the expression on his face told her all she needed to know. Tatjana would not be at the 2016 Olympics in Rio; in fact, there would be no South African female swimmers there.

She smiled bravely, waved to her fans, and made her way back to the changing rooms, where she could let her real emotions out. She was devastated. Maybe she was already past her peak, she thought. It was time to stop.

Meiring came in and sat down quietly beside her. 'We'll get past this,' he said, after a while.

'I don't know what happened.'

'Nothing happened. You did everything right,' he said. 'It's sport – sometimes you win and sometimes you lose.'

'But I did it, just a few weeks ago! Why now, when I really ...' She stopped speaking, not trusting her voice to hold out.

'We'll be back, Tatjana. Trust me. We'll be back. Soon.'

Tatjana and her coach turned their attention

to the Commonwealth Games of 2016 in Brisbane. But first she had to learn to love swimming again. She couldn't let it be only about the results.

During her hours of training in the pool, Tatjana thought about her life and the choices she had made. One day, a memory flashed through her mind. She was running in a 400-metre race at her school sports day. She was in third place, although she knew she could win if she sprinted. But she wasn't sure if she wanted to win or not. If she did, it would feel great, but it would also mean that she would have to miss the upcoming swimming gala, to run in the inter-school athletics meeting.

She had chosen swimming.

Doing the hundreds of kilometres alone in the water, after failing to qualify for the 2016 Olympics in Rio, Tatjana fell in love with the art of swimming again. And at the 2018 Commonwealth Games in Australia, she had the chance to show what she could do.

In the 100-metres breaststroke, she slayed

She had won and set a new African record for the 100 m breaststroke.

the competition, winning gold and setting a new African record of 1:06.41. She slapped the water in delight and threw her arms up in relief.

She also won gold in the 200-metres breaststroke, another African record. Tatjana's wins at the Commonwealth Games helped to wash away the disappointment and doubt that had followed her after her failure to qualify for Rio, and now the Tokyo Olympics were firmly in her sights. She wanted to go faster than any swimmer before her ... and that's exactly what happened.

Tatjana Schoenmaker earned the only South African gold medal at the games, as well as a silver in the 100 metres. In doing so, she demonstrated a remarkable lesson in the power of never giving up.

CHAPTER 11

BLAST FROM THE PAST: LUCAS RADEBE WINS OVER THE LEEDS FANS

Any game against Manchester United at Old Trafford is a big occasion. For Lucas Radebe, the South African centre-back, this game was particularly special. He wanted to prove he was the centre of any defence that he was part of.

Lucas had not had an easy start at Leeds United. There were a few questions about whether he was going to make it, and he struggled to find his place in the Yorkshire team. But the club and the player had worked consistently hard, and people got a taste of his character and commitment to the team.

His confidence was massively boosted by South Africa's historic win at the 1996 African Nations Cup, and the next Premier League season, when Lucas returned, he started to find his groove.

The season was expected to be a great one for Leeds United. They had an excellent squad, and they were going to prove it by starting off well against Manchester United. Leeds were determined to take down the giants. At least, that was the plan.

After fifteen minutes, a long ball forward from Man United caught the Leeds goalkeeper, Mark Beeney, out of position. Beeney raced up to the edge of the box, but he was late, and in desperation he lunged forward with his head and hands to block the attacker. It looked like a foul to everyone in the stadium and the referee calmly pulled out the red card and sent him off.

Leeds were stunned. They were down to ten men after only fifteen minutes, and they had no goalie on the bench. Lucas was the only option.

'Alright, Chief, can you handle this?' asked the coach and Lucas nodded. He was no stranger to goalkeeping. His early career had been between the posts, before Kaizer Chiefs spotted his talent as a defensive player. But being keeper against the 1996 Manchester United team was something else altogether.

He put on the keeper's jersey and gloves and took a few deep breaths as the coach re-organised the defence, and then it was game on, again.

Lucas started well, gathering a few crosses and making some good clearances, but the 'Red Devils' kept on coming. Then some bad luck: the ball bounced nicely and dropped in front of Andy Cole, Manchester United's fearsome striker, who controlled well, and looked up to aim for the net.

Lucas had to make a choice. In a split-second, he chose to run at Cole and get his body in the way. Somehow, Lucas managed to gather the ball. That was scary!

A few moments later, Brain McClair collected a pass on the edge of the Leeds box. Short of a defender, Leeds struggled to shut him down. McClair fired a low shot towards the post, and Lucas dived, pushing it away for a corner.

The Leeds fans went crazy, and Lucas grinned happily.

ROAD TO GLORY

The Leeds fans went crazy, and Lucas grinned happily. He was getting used to this!

At halftime, the score was still 0–0 and the Leeds manager, George Graham, was ecstatic.

'We've got this, lads. They thought we would crumble and fade away but we're still in the game, thanks to the Chief!' He slapped Lucas on the back and the team cheered and clapped.

In the second half, even the talented Ryan Giggs was thwarted by Lucas's goalkeeping gloves, when Lucas dived at the Welshman's feet and plucked the ball away.

Could this really happen? Could ten men and a part-time keeper hold the mighty Man United?

Then in the dying moments of the game, the ball was pinballing around the edge of the Leeds box. It fell to Roy Keane, who moved to his right, beat one man, and fired off a shot. Again, Lucas dived desperately and got a hand to the ball, then pushed it into the side netting, but it was not enough. Goal! One-nil to Manchester United.

Lucas was crestfallen at the defeat, but the wave of support and goodwill that followed the game told him he had finally found a place with Leeds United. This was his home, now. The people of Leeds loved how he had given everything for the team.

The next season, Lucas's leadership ability earned him the position of team captain. The young boy from Soweto, one of eleven children, who had been sent to school in the former homeland of Bophuthatswana, was now the beloved captain of a Premier League team. What a journey!

It was no surprise when Lucas was picked as Leeds United Player of the Year at the end of the season. After that, his career went from strength to strength, and he was selected to lead Bafana Bafana at the 1998 FIFA World Cup in France. Taking the South African team onto the field in the opening game against the hosts was the proudest moment of his life.

France went on to win that tournament. Although the South Africans struggled, they did hold Denmark to a draw.

The next few years were difficult for Lucas. Injuries prevented him from giving his best, and a new crop of young players were determined to replace him. But the man known as 'Rhoo' and 'The Chief' kept leading and motivating. Lucas's style and personality continued to win him fans all over the world.

His ultimate accolade came from Nelson Mandela, who visited the city of Leeds. Standing on the steps of the City Hall, Mandela called Lucas 'my hero'. What an honour and a privilege to receive such praise from Lucas's own personal hero! His beloved game of soccer had truly been good to him.

CHAPTER 12

CHESLIN KOLBE MAKES IT TO THE TOP

Cheslin Kolbe felt his phone vibrating in his pocket. He took it out and smiled when he saw it was his cousin, Wayde van Niekerk.

'Wayde! How are you, man?' he answered. 'Long time no hear.'

'Hey Chessie. Where are you? Sounds like somewhere busy.'

'I'm on the Stormers' bus. Coach is taking us on a three-day camp to Hermanus.'

Siya Kolisi nudged Cheslin. 'Is that Wayde? Tell him I say howzit.'

Cheslin gave Siya a thumbs-up then proceeded to bring his cousin up to date. He was delighted to be invited to join the Stormers camp, going into the 2014 pre-season. It was another step up the professional ladder and this season he was determined to get onto the field for some serious game time.

The first contest of the pre-season was scheduled for 1 February against the Bulls in Polokwane, but the real work kicked off on 22 February, with a game against the Lions.

The Stormers coach, Allister Coetzee, had put together an impressive squad. It was an awesome mix of experienced players – Schalk Burger, Duane Vermeulen, Jean de Villiers and Gio Aplon – alongside some fresh and hungry young talent from the under-21 squad, such as himself, Sikhumbuzo Notshe and Oli Kebble.

'Every time I get out on the field, I can feel my game improving,' he told Wayde.

'That's what happens when you are surrounded by players who are more experienced than you,' Wayde replied.

It was good to catch up on Wayde's news, too. Wayde had been training hard for the 2014 Commonwealth Games in Scotland. He was focusing all his attention on the 400 metres and his training was starting to pay off.

The cousins made a promise to meet up as soon they could, although they knew that it would be some time before either of them could take time out of his schedule.

Hermanus was the perfect place for pre-season fine tuning – not too far from Cape Town, beautiful and quiet with few distractions. The team settled in quickly and got down to work. They had been working hard on their fitness but now it was time to turn their attention towards the more technical aspects of the game. Cheslin was looking forward to getting his skills razor-sharp.

But life doesn't always play ball the way you want it to. In the late afternoon of that first day, Cheslin took a pass low down, scooping the ball up and darting towards a gap. He sidestepped to the right and narrowly avoided a tackle but misjudged the distance from a teammate and they crashed into each other. His foot got caught behind his teammate's leg, and Cheslin felt something in his knee give way as he hit the ground.

A wave of pain and dread rose through his body. Not this. Not now. Not when he was so close to starting to play for the Stormers. But soon the physical agony was all he could think about. The physiotherapist and his teammates crowded around and then picked him up lightly and helped him off the field.

A visibly upset Coetzee told the media that evening that Cheslin needed a small operation and that he would probably be out of action for two months. To have that kind of freak accident just days before the season begins is every coach's worst nightmare.

For Cheslin, it was a crushing blow to miss most of the Super Rugby season, but after he had accepted the fact, he was determined not to sit around and mope. He found ways to keep busy – playing putt-putt with his leg strapped up, visiting the Waterfront, trips to Betty's Bay – and, of course, working out in the gym as much as possible.

Cheslin also discovered that being injured was the perfect time to strike up a romance. He met a beautiful girl called Layla Cupido and the two of them hit it off straight away. Layla was a Capetonian, had attended Pinelands High School and was studying to be a chartered accountant.

By the time he was ready for action again it was late May, and, for the Stormers, it was too late to salvage their participation in the Super Rugby season. They had struggled to build up momentum and crashed out of the competition early.

Next up was South Africa's most important domestic competition, the Currie Cup. With Cheslin back in the mix, the team pulled together and delivered for the fans. They moved like a steamroller through the qualifying rounds, winning eight of the ten games and finishing top of the log.

The Stormers cruised through the quarters and the semis and into the final, where they came up against the Golden Lions. It was going to be a tense game, and the biggest of Cheslin's career so far. In fullback position, he knew that he was going to have to prove himself.

The home crowds had been growing in numbers and enthusiasm with every game. Western Province supporters sang and cheered for every point their team scored. On average, 20 000 fans turned up per game, swelling to over 44 000 people at the final – all waiting to see their heroes lift the trophy.

Walking out onto the field for that final, in front of such a big crowd, was a highly emotional moment for Cheslin.

In the first half, Western Province played well, putting points on the board. Demetri Catrakilis, at flyhalf, converted two penalties in the first ten minutes, and then converted a try in the 36th minute. On the other side of the field, the Lions flyhalf Maritz Boshoff couldn't find his form, missing two kickable attempts that left his team down 13–0 at halftime.

Province started to believe they were going to win it all easily, but the Lions coach must have given his team a tongue-lashing during the break, because the Lions came into the

CHESLIN KOLBE

second half with new determination. Boshoff got an early penalty over, and then his team put together a long string of passes that ended with Jaco van der Walt going over the line in the corner, despite a desperate tackle from Province player Seabelo Senatla.

'Come on, Cheslin! Where's the defence, man?' screamed Allister Coetzee from the sideline.

This was championship rugby – tense, brutal and nerve-racking. Province gave away another penalty, which brought the score to 13–13. The crowd fell silent. Were all the triumphs of the season going to amount to nothing for Western Province?

Jean de Villiers put an arm around Cheslin and urged him to make one final effort.

'We've got this, Ches. We've got this,' said the captain. 'One more big push to end the season on a high note, OK?'

Cheslin nodded, although he was not at all sure. A high ball was kicked towards him, and he saw Lions players rushing forward. But

Cheslin lifted the trophy over his head in front of the crowd.

CHESLIN KOLBE

Cheslin kept his nerve and took the kick well. The crowd clapped in relief. He side-stepped the first opponent and managed to make a few yards, then offloaded the ball.

Slowly the Province team pushed the Lions back into their own half. Cheslin was making a nuisance of himself every time he got the ball. The pressure worked; Province forced an error, got a penalty, and Demetri Catrikilis kicked them into a three-point lead.

With a few minutes to go, the Lions threw all their energy into an attack. Cheslin was exhausted but he kept going. Then a gap opened in the Province defence and the Lions' big hooker, Akker van der Merwe, burst through. To Cheslin, the man looked like a steamroller, but that didn't mean he couldn't take him down.

Cheslin rushed hard at the sprinting hooker, dived low and grabbed him perfectly around the ankles. Down went Van der Merwe, he fumbled the ball and Province players dived onto it.

De Villiers reached down and picked Cheslin up. 'Match-winning tackle, Ches! Well done!' he said, with a massive grin on his face.

A few minutes later it was all over, and Western Province were the Currie Cup champions. Cheslin's whole body ached, but when he lifted the trophy over his head in front of the crowd, the pain melted away. During the tournament, he had scored five tries and one conversion, ending up with 27 points for the season. He pictured his proud parents in the stands, and for a moment, it felt like the sun shone brighter just for him.

CHAPTER 13

ERNST VAN DYK – KING OF THE ROAD

The radio in the car was tuned to a talk station and the presenter was running a quiz.

'Welcome to the show, Cecilia. Are you ready for your first question?'

'Ready,' replied the caller.

'Good,' said the presenter. 'Can you name South Africa's most successful marathon champion of all time?'

'Um … hmmm.'

'Not only has this person won the Boston Marathon an incredible eight times but he or she is on their way back to Boston in the next few days to try and win it again for a record-breaking ninth title.'

The caller was silent while the clock ticked.

'Cecilia?'

'Um ... is it Bruce Fordyce?'

'Nope, sorry. The answer is Ernst van Dyk, the phenomenal wheelchair racer. Next question ...'

In the car, a voice came from the back seat. 'Turn it off, please,' and the taxi driver obliged.

Ernst van Dyk looked out the window as the car rushed towards the airport and tried not to feel disappointment that the caller hadn't known who he was. He tried to shrug the feeling off, but it was painful to be so successful in a sport and yet barely known in your own country.

Since he was a child, Ernst had been incredibly athletic. Both his parents were athletes, and they recognised his gift early on. The difference between him and other children was that Ernst had been born with underdeveloped lower legs that had to be amputated below the knee when he was just a baby. It was the only life he knew, and a lack of legs never stopped him.

He was a great swimmer as a teen and competed in the Barcelona Paralympics in

1992 before finding his true calling, which was wheelchair athletics.

Since then, he had won a gold, two silver and three bronze medals at the Paralympics, but it was really in the marathon that he displayed his talent and stamina. In 2001, he won the Boston Marathon for the first time, in a time of 1:25.12. The following year, he beat that time by two minutes to win again and added a gold in the Los Angeles Marathon and a bronze in the New York Marathon to the list.

And that was just the beginning. The only year Ernst hadn't won the Boston Marathon since 2001 was in 2007. Now, in 2010, he was the undisputed king of the road.

When the taxi dropped him off at the airport, Ernst was struck by a chaotic scene.

'What's going on?' he asked an official.

'There's been a volcanic eruption in Iceland,' the man replied.

'So?'

'A huge cloud has spread all over Europe and all flights are cancelled.'

'But I need to be in Boston in a few days' time. For a race.'

The official shrugged and waved him away so he could deal with the next frustrated passenger.

For the next six days, thousands of people with plans to travel waited for the volcanic cloud to disperse. Ernst worried he was not going to be able to defend his title, but he made it to Boston just in time for the marathon.

On the flight, he had thought about his race strategy. He knew that if he could break away from the pack in the early stages of the race, then gold was his for the taking. Psychologically, it made sense. When a racer sees another competitor far ahead in the lead, sometimes they forget about trying for gold and start competing for second place instead. That was what Ernst wanted.

He put plenty of effort into the first stage of the race and tried to pull away numerous times, but other competitors – in particular, his good friend and rival Krige Schabort – had their own

Ernst barrelled towards the finish line seconds ahead of his rival.

plans and, to his surprise, Ernst found himself falling behind.

But that just motivated him to keep going. He put his head down and pulled harder, pushing himself to perform. Then, with only seven kilometres to go, Ernst realised he was in trouble. Schabort had built up a formidable lead – almost a minute ahead of Ernst – and time was running out.

No more planning or strategy! Now it was just about heart and muscle and who wanted to win the most. When Ernst thought he couldn't possibly dig deeper, he did. And his stamina and determination began to pay off. The distance between him and Schabort dropped to 40 seconds, then 20, then 10. With two kilometres to go, the two athletes were neck and neck.

At the 400-metre mark, Ernst made his final move, going wide on the outside and barrelling towards the finish line, his lungs screaming, to finish four seconds ahead of his lifelong rival.

'That was the hardest race of my life,' he told reporters afterwards. 'I don't think anyone has ever made up a minute in seven kilometres before.'

The win marked his ninth gold medal in Boston. Ernst van Dyk was officially the most successful Boston marathoner of all time.

Back home, Ernst got the recognition he deserved. The president awarded him the Order of Ikhamanga, a special honour granted for outstanding achievements in arts, culture, literature, music, journalism and sports.

For Ernst, it wasn't the end of the road. He continued to dominate the sport until 2016, winning another Boston Marathon gold medal in 2014, and gold at the New York Marathon in 2015. His incredible success proves that no obstacles can stand in the way of true athletic talent and sheer determination.

CHAPTER 14

JANINE VAN WYK REMEMBERS HOW IT ALL BEGAN

Janine van Wyk finished tying up her boots and looked around. She could hardly believe that she was in the changing rooms at Glasgow City stadium, about to play in a 2020 UEFA Women's Champions League match against VfL Wolfsburg from Germany.

The coach blew three short blasts on the whistle and called the players together. He went through a few last notes, making sure they each knew their role, and told them how important this game was. Not that anyone needed reminding. Janine and the rest of the Glasgow City team had trained extremely hard and were determined to give Scottish football a good show for the next ninety minutes.

The two teams lined up in the tunnel and

waited for the game's officials to lead both sides onto the field and get things going. Janine felt like she was acting in a movie. Someone tapped her on the shoulder. She turned around and saw it was an American teammate.

'Playing in a game as big as this reminds me what it was like in the beginning. That excitement when you're a kid. Remember?' her smiling teammate asked. Janine smiled back. Her mind was transported to her childhood, playing soccer on a dirt field in Gauteng. It felt like a different universe, a million miles away.

Janine's mind started to race through her memories, and the journey that had brought her here. Being a female soccer player in a Germiston boys' team during the 1990s had not been easy. She could see it all as if it were happening on a screen in front of her ...

... There was a big blonde boy trapping the ball with his left foot. He had no-one to pass to, so he decided to run towards goal. He tapped the ball forward, skipped past one defender and cut in.

Janine came across to cover the goal. She didn't want the winger to get close enough to shoot, so she launched forward with a sliding tackle and knocked the ball off his toes, just before he shot. Her timing was perfect, and she barely touched the player, but he still went tumbling to the ground.

A stinging pain rose through Janine's leg.

'Ooh that's gonna sting, Janine,' shouted Tommy, the goalkeeper.

They all called it a 'grass burn' but there was hardly any grass on this hard, stony field. She was in agony, but she didn't want to show it. That was one of the unwritten laws when you were the only girl on the playing field. You could never show the boys that you were hurting. They would immediately say things like, 'Typical girl!' or 'Stop acting, Janine!'

She gave the coach a thumbs-up and tried to outrun the pain. The sun was setting behind a big mine dump on the Highveld and the game was nearly over, but her team were still hungry to win. The ball was booted upfield, and everyone chased after it but Janine got to it first, did an expert one-two pass with a teammate, controlled the ball and then shot at goal. The ball hit the post and skidded out for a corner.

The parents who had gathered on the sideline in the freezing Highveld air cheered. Janine went into the box and, when the winger took the corner, the ball fell at her feet, and she stabbed it past the goalkeeper and into the net. What a feeling! Her teammates swamped her and screamed in delight.

After the game, the teams shook hands. She had shown them what she could do. Boys who had given her weird looks in the beginning nodded and said, 'Well done!' All except the centre forward, who had been teasing her throughout the game.

'Not bad. For a girl,' he said as he walked off.

Janine was furious. It wasn't like she was trying to prove a point by playing against boys. There were no girls' teams! What was she supposed to do? 'How would you like it, if there were only girls' teams for you to play in?' she wanted to shout, as she walked off the pitch.

Later that same evening, Janine was at a family braai. The conversation had turned to soccer, just like it always did in this soccer-crazy family. They discussed players, their favourite teams and what had happened in the latest matches.

Janine decided it was the right moment to break her news.

'I have something that I want to tell you,' she said, and it sounded so awkward that everyone at the table fell instantly silent.

'Is everything OK?' asked her mom, fearfully.

'No, it's nothing like that,' said Janine. 'I've ... I just ... I've decided I want to quit the Scaw Metals team.'

'Why, Jay? Did something happen?' asked her dad.

'I want to play on a girls' team. Women's soccer.'

'Why?'

'I've been playing there for ten years, Dad. I'm nearly 15 and if I'm going to make it in women's soccer, I need to play women's soccer.'

'No argument from me! But you know there aren't any teams around here. That's the problem.'

'I've found one,' Janine announced. 'They're called Springs Home Sweepers. They play in Kwa-Thema. It's about thirty kilometres from here.'

'I know where that is,' said her Uncle Mossie. 'But obviously, you know that's a township. You'll be the only white girl on the team.'

Janine shrugged. 'So? Right now, I'm already the odd one out. No difference.' That brought a laugh from everyone.

Soon, they were getting excited about the idea and her parents agreed they would take Janine to try out with Springs Home Sweepers as soon as it was possible to do so.

Sometimes it felt like it was just yesterday when she had driven into Kwa-Thema for the first time. She hadn't been sure what to expect when she got there but the team had gone out of their way to make her feel welcome.

They had joked that she was their 'quota player' or their international star signing, and she had already posed for photos with a number of the players.

'Yho, Janine. Look in the stands! It seems you've already got a following. Normally, no-one bothers to watch our practices.'

She looked around and sure enough, a small crowd of people from Kwa-Thema had turned out to see a blonde, white girl playing soccer. It wasn't a very common sight, especially on a bumpy field in an East Rand township.

Janine felt such relief to be playing in an all-women's soccer team. She was able to compete at a high level without having to prove herself repeatedly. Also, back at Scaw Metals it was fine when they were all kids, but at 15 years old, boys and girls were very different, and she had found herself holding back. Now, she could just play the game ...

... As the teams started walking onto the

Van Wyk went on to become the most capped South African soccer player of all time.

field, a blast of cold Glaswegian air shocked Janine back into the present. She would never forget that Kwa-Thema team and her teammates there, who had become lifelong friends. Springs Home Sweepers had brought her soccer career to life. It had set her on the path to captaining her country, playing at the World Cup, and becoming the most capped South African soccer player of all time.

But now it was time to focus on the UEFA Women's Champions League – as big as it gets in the world of soccer. Janine told herself to stop being nostalgic and focus on the game right in front of her. The referee blew the whistle, the centre forward tapped the ball and once again, it was game on!

CHAPTER 15

QUINTON DE KOCK TAKES THE GLOVES AGAINST SRI LANKA

It was hot and steamy in the dressing room in Galle, before the first cricket Test match in South Africa's July 2014 tour of Sri Lanka.

'It must be thirty degrees already, and we haven't even started the match,' Quinton de Kock muttered.

'Wait until you strap the gloves and pads on,' said AB de Villiers, 'and then you'll know what the word "sweaty" really means.'

'Not too late to change your mind, Abbas,' Quinton replied. 'Just say the word and the gloves are yours.'

AB chuckled. 'You know I'd love to, but my back is saying not this time, thanks. You'll do a great job, Quinnie.'

AB punched him softly on the arm and trotted

down the tunnel to join the rest of the team.

Quinton finished padding up and looked around the changing room. This was a big moment in his career. He had played wicketkeeper in a few limited overs games, but this was his first time behind the stumps in a Test match, and he desperately wanted it to be a success.

He had batted well in the first South African innings and played some big shots to get to his 50, before edging one into the slips off a leg spinner. The team had made 455 and they were positioned to dominate if everything went according to plan in the field.

He slapped his gloves together, took a deep breath and jogged through the stands and onto the field for his wicketkeeping debut.

Sri Lanka started their innings well and raced to 39 before an incredible catch by Vernon Philander down at long leg. Kaushal Silva had tried to hook a bouncer, but he only got a top edge and Big Vern raced in and dived forward to take the catch.

That brought the brilliant Kumar Sangakkara to the wicket, but slowly it emerged that the real danger was on the other end of the wicket. Upul Tharanga was having a great game and was soon up to 83 runs without appearing to make any effort. This was making the bowlers angry.

Hashim Amla, South Africa's captain, had brought JP Duminy on to bowl. Quinton went in close to put Tharanga under pressure. Right then, JP bowled a beauty that made the batsman grope forwards to play it and his back foot slid out of the crease. When he missed the ball, Quinton pounced and gathered it quickly then smashed the stumps to get his first stumping victim in Test cricket!

Duminy jumped into Faf du Plessis's arms and the fielders smothered Quinton as well. The team believed that this was going to change the momentum of the game, and they seemed to be correct when Mahela Jayawardene was dismissed for only three runs. But the next Sri Lankan batsman hung on for one hundred balls until Dale Steyn whipped one down and

Quinton shot out his hand and the ball landed in the pouch perfectly.

Lahiru Thirimanne edged it towards Quinton. He had been so looking forward to this and took the catch easily. AB came running over.

'That's it, Q. Now I can relax out in the field and let you do the work!'

A stumping and a catch and all Quinton's match nerves disappeared. He got another two catches as the Sri Lankans limped along to end on 292 all out. Quinton felt he hadn't played too badly for a first time.

In the second innings, the Proteas tried to score much quicker so they could build up a big total and have plenty of time to bowl at the Sri Lankans. Quinton made 36 off 40 balls and was happy with that.

What he was really looking forward to, was getting back behind the stumps.

He had always loved playing wicketkeeper, right back to when he was part of the King Edward VII High School First XI. One of his favourite cricket memories was when he made his T20 debut against New Zealand on 21 December 2012. Not only had he scored a quick 28 runs, but he had also taken two catches behind the stumps.

In the last few months, Quinton had been doing a lot of work with veteran keeper Mark Boucher and it was paying off. He wanted to be known as not just a batsman, but an all-rounder.

If they could win this match against Sri Lanka, it would be a big victory for the Proteas. They had only beaten Sri Lanka twice in Test matches and they knew they could do much better. They went out to field with a lead of 369, which the team felt they could defend.

The first hour of the second innings was a dream for Quinton. Dale Steyn was bowling beautifully and causing all sorts of problems for the opening batsmen. He bowled one that teased the outside off stump and Tharanga threw the bat at it and got an edge. Quinton launched himself to his left and managed to hold on to it to get the first wicket.

Then Dale Steyn bowled the perfect length to Silva and got him to poke forward. The ball shot off the bat towards him. It was pure instinct. Quinton shot out his hand, and somehow the ball landed in the pouch perfectly. He had both the opening batsmen and Sri Lanka was on the ropes.

Things just kept getting better. It was one of those games that you remember for a long time. Quinton ended up with five wickets, and it would have been six if he hadn't dropped an easy one when he lost concentration. But this didn't make a difference in the end, and South Africa won by 135 runs.

After the match, Amla ran over and shook his hand and then the coach told him he had solved the question of what to do about AB's workload.

Quinton had always been a team player and to know that he was an important part of the national cricket team felt amazing. And being able to excel at something that he loved so much was the cherry on top.

CHAPTER 16

FAF DE KLERK STEERS A JAW-DROPPING SPRINGBOK COMEBACK

In the world of sports, there are few games as popular as a rugby Test match between South Africa and England at Ellis Park. Faf de Klerk was beyond excited to be part of one. He desperately wanted to cement his place in the team and play in the 2019 World Cup in Japan.

The team was fired up to play well for their new coach, Rassie Erasmus. It was his first big Test and everyone wanted to do well for him. But it was going to be a huge challenge.

England were ranked fourth in the world at that time and had been improving steadily under the guidance of coach Eddie Jones. The team had been unbeaten throughout 2016, had won the Six Nations Championship in 2016 and 2017 and had recently equalled the world record of 18 games undefeated.

In the first minute of the game, Faf de Klerk fed the ball out to RG Snyman, who gathered it cleanly, then went to ground. He jumped right back in, got the ball out and passed it to flyhalf Handré Pollard, who was tackled hard. Jean-Luc du Preez charged into the ruck, but he conceded a penalty.

It was a massive 61 metres to the posts, but the England fullback Elliot Daly wasn't worried, and in the thin Highveld air the ball soared high, then dropped just over the posts to give England three precious points in the first two minutes of the game.

Following the restart, the Boks were quickly forced back onto defence. England whipped the ball down their advancing backline with a series of quick passes until it was in the hands of winger Mike Brown, who beat two tackles and bundled it over into the corner for an England try.

Daly sent the ball back over the posts with

his second kick of the match and, in the first five minutes of the game, the Springboks found themselves already down by ten points and staring defeat in the face.

Finally, the Springboks were able to mount an attack, which led to a penalty that Pollard converted. But the English stormed back and the Springbok defence was leaking badly. Another series of neat passes ended with Daly, who sliced through the defence like a knife carving fresh Springbok biltong.

'Another beautifully constructed England try,' announced the South African television commentator grudgingly. Faf was stunned and unsure what to do.

Silence settled over the stadium. The fans had come to see a fresh start for Springbok rugby, but it appeared they would be getting a bruising defeat, with a side order of humiliation, instead.

The try was converted easily, and the scoreboard broadcast the shame to anyone brave enough to look up: 17–3 to the visitors with over

Faf de Klerk was having the game of his life.

an hour left to play. The untested Springbok team was now facing overwhelming odds, and England were fired up.

The hits just kept on coming.

England won some more possession following a breakdown on the halfway line. The flyhalf George Ford spotted Jonny May charging down the wing and floated a perfect high pass that left three Springbok defenders flat-footed. May collected the ball in one easy motion and charged forward before flipping an inside pass to the captain, Owen Farrell, who cantered over easily for England's third try.

Fifteen minutes into the game and 21 points down, the Springboks were embarrassed and unsure of how to respond. Faf spotted a few spectators packing up and leaving.

The overworked scoreboard ticked up again, registering 24 points to 3.

They needed a spark ... and then it happened.

After Faf passed the ball to a teammate in the 18th minute, the huge English lock forward Maro Itoje jumped on him and refused to let

FAF DE KLERK

him up. The game was carrying on, his team needed him, but Itoje lay on Faf, smothering him, and it made Faf furious.

This is not how this game is going to go, he told himself.

One minute later, the Springboks were in a good attacking position down the right wing. Sbu Nkosi charged hard at the defence, going down just metres from the corner flag. The ball popped out of the ruck and Faf waited a few seconds before picking it up. He spotted Itoje make a mistake, lose his footing and tumble to the ground. Now there was a small gap. Faf burst through it and hurled himself towards the tryline just a few metres away. Despite two pairs of strong arms trying to hold him back, he wriggled free and dotted the ball down on the line. Try to the Springboks!

Faf gave Itoje a little shove and a wink. They were back in business. It was 24–8, and a sense of relief rolled across the stadium like thunder from a Highveld storm.

Ten minutes later, Nkosi was prowling

on the wing, waiting for an opportunity. Faf picked the ball up, broke through a tackle and offloaded to Damian de Allende, who beat his man and handed off to Nkosi. Nkosi accelerated towards the line, but he was being hustled hard, so he dropped the ball onto his right foot, punted it gently forward over the try line and chased it. Daly, the England fullback, came charging in at speed but overshot the ball and it bobbled enticingly in the end zone for Nkosi, who just managed to drop a hand onto it and score his first try for the Boks.

Another great try started by Faf de Klerk.

And just like that it became a different game. Momentum had swung 180 degrees. The Springboks had found their confidence again and nothing would keep them back now.

Itoje was sticking to Faf, harassing and fouling him when he could get away with it, but Faf was unfazed. In the 33rd minute, he sent the ball down the line to Nkosi, who combined with another debutant, Aphiwe Dyantyi, to go over the line for a beautiful third try.

FAF DE KLERK

The Boks were back within four points of the lead. It was England's turn to look shell-shocked. The relief in the stadium had turned to excitement and then into certainty that South Africa could win.

Faf de Klerk was having the game of his life. Two minutes before halftime, he picked up the ball from the base of the scrum, accelerated and combined with Pollard, who offloaded a long pass to fullback Willie le Roux. Nkosi was right there in case he was needed, but Le Roux had transformed into a freight train crashing over the line to score. From the earlier 24–3 score, the Boks went into halftime 29–27, two points ahead of England.

'That was one of the greatest 40 minutes in Test history,' shouted a commentator. 'Fifty-six points in 40 minutes!'

Faf was pleased. He knew he had done his job as playmaker on the team. Even though there were still 40 minutes to go, he knew that his team wasn't going to give up now. They had worked too hard to get back into the game.

ROAD TO GLORY

And he was right. The Boks held on to win the game 42–39. Faf knew for a fact he was going to the 2019 World Cup.

CHAPTER 17

AKANI SIMBINE RACES TOWARDS THE TITLE OF 'WORLD'S FASTEST MAN'

Tokyo Olympics, 100 metres, gold medal: that was the plan for the young South African sprinter Akani Simbine. For the last few years, Akani had done everything he could to prepare well for the Games, which were scheduled for late July 2020. This was going to be the year he would be named the fastest runner in the world.

But life had other plans for all of us. COVID-19 raced around the world faster than any sprinter, and claimed millions of lives, jobs and dreams along the way.

Akani's year had started so well. In February at the University of Johannesburg stadium, he ran a 150-metre race in 15.08 seconds, which was a South African record. But the world doesn't pay much attention to that strange, middle-of-nowhere race. All eyes focus on the 100-metre and 200-metre races.

Up next was a prestigious 100-metre event at the Tuks stadium, University of Pretoria. Moments before the race, Akani's coach, Werner Prinsloo, took him aside for a chat.

'I've got an odd feeling today,' said the coach.

'What is it?'

'It just feels like this might be the last race we run for a while.'

'Why do you say that? The Olympics are only a few months away.'

'This virus is bad, Akani, and it's getting worse. Every day events are being cancelled.'

Akani looked down the track and stretched out his calf muscles. His whole career he had known what he needed to do to get ahead. But this was completely out of his control.

'So, what are you saying, coach?' he asked.

'Give it everything you've got today. This is no longer a warm-up race. This needs to be the one.'

Akani nodded and focused on the race. Ten minutes later, he was on the starting blocks and staring down the track. At the gun, he exploded out of the blocks and was into his full stride in seconds, arms pumping, head still and legs pounding the track. He didn't let off the heat for a millisecond, until he was all the way across the line.

In 9.91 seconds it was all over. Prinsloo was delighted.

'That's what I'm talking about!' he yelled. 'The fastest time anyone in the world has run this year! Now they know who to watch at the Olympics!'

Akani was proud and thrilled, but his joy didn't last long. Bad news about COVID-19 was everywhere, and sure enough, a few weeks later the whole country went into a complete lockdown. All competitive sport was stopped, the gyms were closed, and people were only allowed out of their homes to buy food and other essentials.

Internationally, the same thing was happening. The Olympic Games were postponed, and no-one knew what was going to happen next.

It was scary and difficult for everyone, but for professional athletes like Akani Simbine it was agony. He longed to train. He dreamt about running. The days of lockdown turned into weeks and then months.

Akani, like so many others, had never felt lower in his life. But eventually, in July 2020, the athletics track at the University of Pretoria reopened. The first morning they were able to go out and run slowly around the track in the crisp winter air was a wonderful feeling of freedom.

Akani got straight back to work, training harder than ever and determined to put the delays behind him.

A few weeks later Akani and Prinsloo arrived at the airport ahead of their first big European championship of the season. They were both determined that Akani would perform.

'Europe better be ready for us, Akani,' said Prinsloo.

Akani focused on just one thing – the finish line.

'Exactly. It's time to lay down a marker for next year's Olympics. After all, the Games were just postponed, not cancelled,' Akani agreed.

Akani kept his eyes on the prize. Over the next few weeks, he dominated the European track circuit, winning the 100-metre race in big track meets in France, Italy and Spain. They were good victories, but they were all just over ten seconds, and Akani wanted to reduce his time again.

The final race of the series was at the Rome Diamond League. In that race, his great rival, Arthur Cissé of Ivory Coast, got off to a flying start. Akani thought he had lost him. But he pushed hard, and his body responded. They were neck and neck, with 15 metres to go, but a surging finish saw Akani just make it over the line ahead of Cissé.

That was the kind of competition he needed, and when he looked up at the stopwatch it read 9.96 seconds. Perfect.

Alongside the solo adventures of the 100 metres, Akani focused his attention on being part of the relay team. He loved the group dynamic, and that year, South Africa had an unusually strong relay team in Thando Dlodlo, Clarence Munyai, Tlotliso Leotlela and him. They set their sights on the 2021 World Athletics Relay Championships in Poland in early May.

'All the best are going to be there,' said Munyai.

'Yup. The Brazilians are looking strong,' agreed Akani.

'Even France and Italy are quick this year,' said Dlodlo. 'It's going to be tight.'

The team worked hard on their changeovers and their individual performances until they were sure they would be a force in the race. Everyone knew that relays often involved a bit of good luck: the fastest team could be derailed by a bad changeover on the day, or a foot over the line, which led to disqualification. That was part of the game.

The weather was cold in Poland on 1 May. It was only 11 degrees when the South African team lined up for their heat. They executed the race perfectly; no mistakes, and they didn't exhaust themselves, either. They qualified in a time of 38.49 seconds, which was third fastest on the day, behind Italy and Brazil.

The team were super pumped up the following day as they prepared for the finals. They knew that they could win the race.

The cold weather that day meant nothing to Dlodlo, who was first off the blocks for South Africa. He completed the first leg in 10.83, slightly off the leading pace. When Leotlela took over, they were in fifth place, but Leotlela's 9.16 time catapulted them into second, behind Italy. As Munyai took over for the third leg, Brazil burst to the front and the Italian challenge collapsed.

Akani's heart was pounding as he waited. Come on! But it seemed Brazil was just too far ahead. When he got the baton, he was already three metres behind. But quickly Akani found his rhythm, pumping his arms and legs, and focused on just one thing – the finish line.

Somehow, in only ten seconds, he clawed his way back to the front. The Brazilian runner was stunned as they crossed the line together. How could he have blown that lead?

It was an incredible race, and no-one knew who had won as they crossed the line. All eyes were on the photo finish – and yes, there it was! South Africa in first place. They had done it. The team clocked 38.71 and took the gold. Akani was smothered by his ecstatic teammates, who were screaming with happiness!

Only one year earlier, COVID-19 had them all confined to their homes and unable to run. Now here they were with gold medals and all the confidence in the world to go into the delayed Olympic Games in Tokyo. Nothing would stand in their way.

CHAPTER 18

BLAST FROM THE PAST: JOSIA THUGWANE WINS GOLD FOR MADIBA

At 25 years old, Josia Thugwane had come a long, long way. Josia was born in a small farming town called Bethal, had little schooling to his name, and was employed by a coal mine. Now here he was, standing in the pack of runners on the starting line for the marathon at the 1996 Atlanta Olympics, about to run for South Africa in the last event of the Games.

Josia didn't know whether he could win, but he knew he was there because of Nelson Mandela, the man who had liberated his country and delivered free and fair elections in 1994. He was going to run his best to honour his president.

He was part of a formidable trio of South

JOSIA THUGWANE

African marathon runners. Lawrence Peu and Gert Thys had both performed better than Josia had in the competitions leading up to the Olympics. In fact, the time Josia had run to win the national title had been just outside the qualifying time required, but the Olympic authorities had relaxed the rules as he was national champion.

It was early morning, but the Atlanta air was warm and humid. As he stood there, Josia felt that everyone was equal at that moment. They were all flesh and blood and any one of the more than 120 runners could win the event over the next two hours.

There had been some encouraging performances from his South African teammates, particularly in the swimming pool. Penny Heyns had won gold in the 100-metres and 200-metres breaststroke events, and Marianne Kriel had won bronze at backstroke. On the track, Hezekiel Sepeng had run brilliantly to win a silver medal in the 800-metres race.

Still, no black South African had ever won

an Olympic gold before. This would be the last chance for another four years to put that right. And the 150 thousand rands prize money that the government was offering for a gold medal would change his life forever.

Josia reflected on how it was almost a miracle that he was there at all. Only five months earlier, he had been shot in the face and then jumped out of a moving car to escape from a trio of hijackers who were trying to steal the car he was driving. Luckily, the bullet had just passed between his lip and chin and not done too much damage. But the jump from the car had injured his back and he had needed intensive therapy seven days a week to be available for today's race.

The gun fired, and Josia started well, settling into an easy rhythm. The full pack of runners did three laps of the Olympic stadium before heading out into the streets. The first big break came at the 16-kilometre mark, when about fifty runners broke away from the pack and moved up a gear. These were the runners who were expected to challenge for a medal.

When he was younger, Josia had run marathons without even knowing how long they were supposed to be. Now he was experienced; this was his 19th race, and he knew that timing was everything. He stayed patient.

The South African team felt good and were happy to push hard. At the 25-kilometre point, all three South Africans raced to the front and stayed there, leaving the rest of the pack confused and unsure of how to react. They didn't know much about South African running – what should they do? Even the commentators on TV battled to pronounce the runners' names.

One runner who saw the danger and responded well was Lee Bong-ju of South Korea. He caught up with the South Africans and stayed with them, eventually overtaking Peu and Thys when they fell back.

With about ten kilometres to go, it started to look like a three-way race between Josia, Bong-ju and a Kenyan youngster, Erick Wainaina. The lead kept changing between

With that kind of courage and determination, he was certain to win.

the three of them. Then, with less than five kilometres to go, Lee stormed back to the front and tried to get away.

The crowd was filling up the Olympic stadium to see the finish. Back in South Africa, people crowded around televisions and radios to see if their hero could make a dream come true.

Josia felt good. There was no pain, and he still had some gas left in his tank. With just a couple of kilometres to go, he made his move, pushing past Lee and striding to the front as he ran into the stadium. But neither of the challengers was willing to let go of the golden dream, and as the trio started the last four hundred metres around the track, after 42 kilometres of running, there was less than twenty metres separating them.

Josia felt that his whole life had been leading to this moment – from running barefoot in the veld to running here, the pride of his nation. He wanted and needed the gold, and he knew he had the courage and determination to do it.

Josia put his head down and charged, crossing the finish line in 2:12.36, only three seconds ahead of Bong-ju, who took silver, while Wainaina took bronze. An Olympic gold for South Africa! And Josia was the first black South African to have this honour.

Tears of joy and pride flowed across the country. The South African national anthem, played at the closing ceremony of the 1996 Olympic Games, was a sign to the world that the dark days of apartheid had truly ended, and the country could look forward to a brighter future.

SOURCES

CHAPTER 1: https://www.npr.org/2018/07/13/628880059/game-set-marathon-anderson-wins-record-shattering-wimbledon-semifinal

CHAPTER 2: https://www.news24.com/citypress/news/winning-women-bongiwe-msomi-from-filler-to-captain-20201115; https://www.uj.ac.za/newandevents/Pages/Proteas-captain-Bongiwe-Msomi-appointed-as-head-coach-of-UJ-Netball.aspx

CHAPTER 3: https://www.golfcentraldaily.com/2015/07/flashback-louis-oosthuizens-red-dot.html

CHAPTER 4: https://mg.co.za/article/2015-09-17-luvo-manyonga-jumps-or-dies/; http://www.firstpost.com/sports/how-luvo-manyonga-overcame-drug-addiction-to-become-an-olympic-medallist-and-role-model-4234037.html

CHAPTER 5: *Road to Glory: Caster Semenya* by Jeremy Daniel. Published 2018, Jonathan Ball

CHAPTER 6: *Road to Glory: Percy Tau* by Jeremy Daniel. Published 2019, Jonathan Ball

CHAPTER 7: https://athleticsweekly.com/athletics-news/sunette-viljoen-life-less-ordinary-57465/

CHAPTER 8: https://www.sacricketmag.com/114845-2/

CHAPTER 9: *Road to Glory: Chad le Clos* by Jeremy Daniel. Published 2019, Jonathan Ball

CHAPTER 10: https://www.news24.com/sport/othersport/olympics2020/meet-the-coaching-mind-behind-tatjana-schoenmakers-meteoric-rise-20210731; https://olympics.com/en/featured-news/african-breaststroke-queen-tatjana-schoenmaker-is-ready-to-cause-an-upset-in-tok

CHAPTER 11: https://www.planetfootball.com/nostalgia/a-forensic-analysis-of-lucas-radebe-playing-in-goal-against-man-utd/; https://thesefootballtimes.co/2020/03/03/lucas-radebe-from-being-shot-in-south-africa-to-national-icon-and-leeds-legend/

CHAPTER 12: *Road to Glory: Cheslin Kolbe* by Jeremy Daniel. Published 2021, Jonathan Ball

CHAPTER 13: https://en.wikipedia.org/wiki/Ernst_van_Dyk; https://www.laureus.co.za/project/ernst-van-dyk/

CHAPTER 14: https://ewn.co.za/2020/07/14/janine-van-wyk-signs-for-scottish-champions; https://www.

heraldscotland.com/sport/18592282.glasgow-city-move-allows-janine-van-wyk-chance-fulfill-champions-league-ambition/

CHAPTER 15: https://www.iol.co.za/sport/cricket/proteas/ab-must-hang-up-his-gloves-1442930

CHAPTER 16: *Siya Kolisi: Against All Odds* by Jeremy Daniel. Published 2019, Jonathan Ball

CHAPTER 17: https://www.dailymaverick.co.za/article/2021-07-29-team-sa-sprinter-akani-simbine-brimming-with-confidence-ahead-of-100m-olympic-race/

CHAPTER 18: http://www.espn.com/espn/feature/story/_/id/13340173/once-lauded-nelson-mandela-former-olympian-josia-thugwane-forgotten-south-africa

AUTHOR'S NOTE

The events in this book are based on fact. However, I have taken creative licence in certain scenes with dialogue, timelines and some detail in the interests of creating stories that are entertaining and fun for young readers. I have tried to stay true to the character and life story of each of the subjects, based on the known facts, and to celebrate their achievements.

ALSO AVAILABLE IN THE
ROAD TO GLORY
SERIES

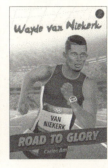
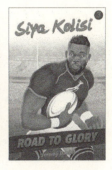